PUSSYCATS

PUSSYCATS
a photographic celebration

MQP
MQ Publications Ltd

A cat is only technically

an animal, being divine.

Robert Lynd

To understand a cat, you must realize that

he has his own gifts, his own viewpoint,

even his own morality.

Lilian Jackson Braun

When the tea is brought at five o'clock,

And all the neat curtains are drawn with care,

The little black cat with bright green eyes

Is suddenly purring there.

"Saki" (Hector Hugh Munro)

His friendship is not easily won but

it is something worth having.

Michael Joseph

To get on with animals you

must have a sense of humor.

"Saki" (Hector Hugh Monro)

In a cat's eyes,

all things belong to cats.

English Proverb

How do you spell mousetrap

in three letters?

Riddle

No matter how much cats fight,

there always seems to be plenty

of kittens.

Abraham Lincoln

Cats are a mysterious kind of folk.

There is more passing in their

mind than we are aware of.

Sir Walter Scott

Mice amused him, but he usually considered them too small game to be taken seriously; I have seen him play for an hour with a mouse and then let him go with a royal condescension.

Charles Dudley Warner

You could never accuse him of

idleness, and yet he knew the

secret of repose.

Charles Dudley Warner

You will always be lucky if you

know how to make friends with

strange cats.

Colonial American Proverb

Cats are dainty patricians,

whereas dogs, whatever their

social status, retain a

parvenu's lack of cleanliness,

and are irredeemably vulgar.

Pierre Loti

Idling has always been my

strong point. I take no

credit to myself—it is a gift.

Jerome K. Jerome

The cat is a dilettante in fur.

Theophile Gautier

The smallest feline is a masterpiece.

Leonardo da Vinci

A cat is more intelligent

than people believe, and

can be taught any crime.

Mark Twain

The cat is the only

non-gregarious

domestic animal.

Francis Galton

The most unsociable cat, when it finds itself

wrapped up in someone's coat and put to

sleep upon his bed—stroked, fed, and tended

with every imaginable care—soon ceases to

stand upon its dignity.

Murasaki Shikibu

The cat and dog may kiss,

yet are none the better friends.

Proverb

Cats are absolute individuals, with their own ideas

about everything, including the people they own.

John Digman

If cats could talk, they would lie to you.

Rob Kopack

He lies there, purring and dreaming, shifting

his limbs now and then in an ecstasy of

cushioned comfort. He seems the incarnation

of everything soft and silky and velvety, without

a sharp edge in his composition, a dreamer

whose philosophy is sleep and let sleep.

"Saki" (Hector Hugh Munro)

My cat has taken to mulled port and rum punch. Poor old dear! He is all the better for it.

Jerome K. Jerome

Cat: a pygmy lion who loathes mice, hates

dogs, and patronizes human beings.

Oliver Herford

A cat improves the garden

wall in sunshine, and the

hearth in foul weather.

Judith Merkle Riley

61

Cats allow us to love them,

for which we should be duly grateful.

Anne Taylor Brown

Cats are intended to teach us

that not everything in nature

has a function.

Anonymous

Her function is to sit and be admired.

Georgina Strickland Gates

Cats are like Baptists.

They raise hell

but you can't

catch them at it.

Anonymous

My little grandson is a darling,

but he can never take the place of

my cats.

Anonymous

Cats use their voices much as

a means of expression.

Charles Darwin

73

My cat is a lion in a jungle of small bushes.

English Proverb

All your wondrous wealth of hair,

Dark and fair,

Silken-shaggy, soft and bright

As the clouds and beams of night,

Pays my reverent hand's caress

Back with friendlier gentleness.

Algenon Charles Swinburne

Since each of us is blessed with only one life,

why not live it with a cat?

Robert Stearns

A kitten is the delight of

a household. All day long

a comedy is played by

this incomparable actor.

Jules Chapfleury

Like a graceful vase, a cat, even

when motionless, seems to flow.

George F. Will

Cats seem to go on the

principle that it never

does any harm to ask

for what you want.

Joseph Wood Krutch

Thou art the Great Cat, the avenger of the Gods, and the judge of words, and the president of the sovereign chiefs and the governor of the holy circle; thou art indeed...the Great Cat.

Inscription on the Royal Tombs at Thebes

Dogs come when they're called; cats take a message and get back to you later.

Mary Bly

The cat is domestic only as

far as it suits its own ends.

"Saki" (Hector Hugh Munro)

There is no need for a piece of

sculpture in a home that has a cat.

Wesley Bates

The best exercise for a

cat is another cat.

Jo and Paul Loeb

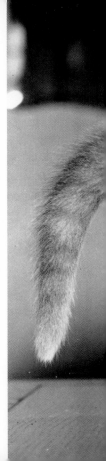

A kitten is so flexible that she is

almost double...

Henry David Thoreau

All animals except man know that the principal

business of life is to enjoy it.

Samuel Butler

Cats consider theft a game

And whosoever you may blame

Refuse the slightest sign of shame.

Anonymous

A house without a cat, and a well-fed,

well-petted and properly revered cat,

may be a perfect house, perhaps, but

how can it prove its title?

Mark Twain

A cat's a cat and that's that.

American Folk Saying

Picture Credits

cover: A kitten is surrounded by milk bottles bigger than he is, 1964.

title page: "Maudsley," a kitten, 1978.

page 4: A sleeping kitten wearing a miniature crown, circa 1950.

page 7: A kitten takes a swipe at three goldfish in a bowl, circa 1950.

page 8: Paddy the cat with his paw in the milk jug on the tea tray, 1923.

page 11: Actor Oliver Reed reading through a script watched by his cat, Felix, 1960.

page 12: A kitten, a duckling, and a cup and saucer, circa 1955.

page 15: City cats watching as the "cat's meat man" cuts up their food, 1939.

page 16: A cat hangs a row of tame rats on the washing line to dry, 1933.

page 18: Blue Persian kittens at the home of Mrs I. Speers, London, 1931.

page 21: A cat sat next to a "No Fishing" sign in a garden in Weston-Super-Mare, 1937.

page 23: A pedigree Siamese kitten that was sold for 100 dollars and imported into the USA, 1949.

page 25: A 77-year-old cat celebrates her birthday in style, 1997.

page 26: Portrait of an elderly fisherman playing a whistle with a cat sitting on his shoulder, circa 1935.

page 28: Domestic bliss: a boxer and a kitten share a saucer of milk, 1972

page 31: A cat being lowered in a basket, 1933.

page 32: Anita Ekberg plays the glamorous Sylvia in "La Dolce Vita." In this scene she holds a tiny kitten in her hands, 1960.

page 35: "Maudsley," a kitten, 1978.

page 36: A cat and his young mistress examine the catch from their joint fishing trip, 1937.

page 38: Children at the Chelsea Hostel for children, in London, sitting on a wall beside a cat, 1932.

page 41: Whisky the cat "baby" sitting, 1954.

page 42: A basset hound cleaning behind the ears of a kitten, circa 1950.

page 44: A cat balancing on the shoulder of an RAF pilot, circa 1944.

page 47: Two cats sitting in a domestic referigerator, 1976.

page 48: The whiskered face of a sleeping cat, 1929.

page 51: Prizewinning Blue Persian "Champion Foxburrow Faery" in his travel basket ready for a trip to Manchester to compete in a cat show, 1955.

page 53: A kitten stretches and yawns at the Greenwich Village Humane Cat League in New York, circa 1950.

page 54: English film actress Ann Todd with a blue Persian cat she bought in Scotland, 1935.

Published by MQ Publications Limited
12 The Ivories, 6-8 Northampton Street, London N1 2HY
Tel: 020 7359 2244 / Fax: 020 7359 1616
email: mail@mqpublications.com

Copyright © MQ Publications Limited, 2002

ISBN: 184072-168-5

1 3 5 7 9 0 8 6 4 2

Cover Design: John Casey
Design: Alexia Smith
Series Editor: Elizabeth Carr

Printed and bound in China